GU00857714

How to ~~Write a~~
Groom's Speech

The Definitive Step by Step Guide

STEVE JAMES

ISBN-13: 978-1543084726

ISBN-10: 1543084729

For all the grooms who don't know where to start.

CONTENTS

ACKNOWLEDGMENTS

Permission for the photographs for this book has been kindly provided by **Rob Tarren Photography**. You can visit Rob's website at www.robtarren.co.uk.

Thanks to Jacqui, Marie and Pav for being my co-editors by proof-reading this book. I really appreciate your support.

Finally, thanks to my wife, Rach, for everything.

Chapter One

Introduction – My story

It can feel daunting when you start writing your groom's speech, staring at a blank page with accumulating dread. This book will guide you in writing your personalized groom's speech from start to finish.

I wanted to make my speech immaculate, so therefore I put lots of effort into planning a template. I drafted and re-drafted my template three times. This preparation made the reading and the delivery of my groom's speech very easy. It's a fantastic feeling to have close friends and family congratulate you afterwards, and this book will get you there!

My greatest fear was that I missed thanking someone through careless planning. I felt that having a longer than usual speech was a small price to pay, and completely worth it. If you want to deliver a shorter speech, you can easily take the best bits from this template and shorten it.

As you have bought this book to assist you, you have taken a step that 99% of grooms won't! I know that you are committed to make the best speech possible and are prepared to put in the effort. For this you should be commended.

As it would turn out, at my wedding we had five soon-to-be-wed couples who were our guests. Within a month of giving my groom's speech, I had requests from some grooms-to-be to help them with their speeches! After sending them my speech and offering advice, I realized that I could help many more people around the world by putting all of my work into this book.

This book provides you with a guide and template to create a groom's speech to be proud of. Have a pen and paper ready (or your laptop open) and get ready to write your speech by following my step-by-step guide. I recommend you work through the chapters one-by-one and let me help you by explaining how of my own speech went, with some gems of advice along the way.

Following this one section at a time allows you to work on your speech at a pace that suits you. This way you can take the time to pick up where you left off. I have dropped in my best bits of advice from my own experience, which will explain what made it a success! I shall act as your secret mentor throughout the process, and give you my tips and insights.

One more thing; when you have planned your speech, make sure you share your own experiences with other soon-to-be grooms. They will thank you for it!

Happy writing,

Steve.

Chapter Two

What should the groom's speech include?

There are two essential things a groom must do in his speech:

1) Say thanks to the relevant people
2) Tell his wife how much he loves her!

If you do these two things alone, you will get lots of 'Ahh's, of acceptance and love.

Traditionally, the main three speeches at a wedding are from:

- The father of the bride
- The groom
- The best man

There are some exceptions to this rule due to absences and the scale of your wedding, but most weddings with a sit-down meal will include these three.

Father of the bride's speech

The father of the bride's speech traditionally precedes the groom's speech. His speech will definitely have some anecdotes about his daughter from throughout her life, and say how beautiful she looks on the day. This is usually followed by a joke or two about how the groom met the bride's family, how the groom has taken his pride and joy from him, or even how the groom drink's all his beer when he visits! Overall his speech is brief, endearing and will allow you to get a feel for the audience for your speech to come.

His speech will always end with a toast to the happy couple' or 'bride and groom'. It's worth speaking to the father of the bride beforehand if possible, as some people like to keep their speech a secret until the day. It is worth asking them so you can cross-check material with your own speech to make sure you are not covering too much of the same ground. If the three main speeches flow from one to the other without too much repetition it makes the experience for the guests more interesting and engaging.

Look around at who is seated where for if you need to address people during your speech. It's as if you have sent a crash test dummy in for a trial run to test the audience! As he is the first to address the guests, it really is up to him to open up proceedings.

You can get a feel for which of his jokes go down well and how his vocals come over on the microphone. Make sure that in your speech you give thanks for his kind words; this will transition well into your speech. It is good to have a joined up approach to all the speeches, rather than give each speech as a separate episode.

Groom's speech

The groom's speech itself should be a tribute to a groom's love for his wife, and is an opportunity to say thank you to everyone that needs thanking. The groom should toast both the bridesmaids and the bride. The groom, traditionally, may wish to thank the host, the in laws, his parents and the groom's party, which I did and will reveal how.

Some brides may wish to take the opportunity (during your groom's speech) to toast the bridesmaids herself. My wife was happy to allow me to do the honours!

Chapter Three

How to make an outline plan of your speech

This section is for all those looking for a starting point. I found the best way to get creative is have a basic structure to turn to. This structure can be shortened or lengthened, but will consist of the basic format:

- Welcome and General Opening
- Thanks to New In-laws (Mother and Father of the bride)
- Thanks to Own Mother and Father
- Thanks to Maid of Honour and Bridesmaids
- Thanks to Grooms Party
- Thanks to Pageboys, Flower Girls and Venue
- Speech about your Wife
- Introduction of Best Man

I used this exact structure for my groom's speech, which is detailed in the next chapter. Each section will be explained in the chapters that follow. At a minimum, this bullet point list is all you need for your speech and could be put on a sticky note!

I've never felt like a natural public speaker, especially not in front of friends and family, but by following this process I was able to convince everyone I was calm, relaxed and knew what I was doing. I used my skills as a teacher to plan and execute my speech, and have put all my efforts into this book so you can reap the benefits!

I felt that I needed to have my speech written down word for word. By the end of this book, once you have written your speech you may feel like you know it well enough to write shorthand notes, or even write it on bullet points on a scrap of paper! If this is you then by all means go ahead, but my process of planning will make you understand what you are trying to say and how you can actually say it.

You need to remember that everyone in the room is on your side, and that you will never have a more supportive audience. Guests will whoop, clap and encourage you, so be prepared for it!

My speech was after the wedding breakfast (meal). After a few drinks, the guests were in great spirits and were nice and relaxed! I chose to read from the sheets as I had a lot of people to thank and did not want to feel stuck for words. This made my speech slightly longer, but was a price I was happy to pay for getting my speech right and not missing any detail.

If you put yourself in the position of a guest at your wedding, they will be sitting at their table sipping their drink, looking around the room and maybe whispering to others on their table. Although you might feel like everyone's attention is on you, most guests are actually passive listeners and let their attention wander. I was grateful for a microphone provided by the venue, so it's worth checking if you have access to one. A microphone allows you to speak, not shout. With this in mind I felt my delivery could be calm, relaxed and yet still be heard by everyone using my usual speaking voice.

A good piece of advice from another groom I talked to recently was to walk around. He felt his knees were starting to shake from underneath him through nervousness. He found that pacing gently at the front of the venue helped him control this. It will depend on if you are on a traditional top table or not, as this will restrict you a little, but if you have an open floor there's no harm in owning the space. It gives off the aura that you are confident. However, I don't advise you do laps of the venue as it isn't stand-up comedy.

The groom will mostly speak on behalf of his wife and himself, but when he speaks to or about his bride he should speak for himself alone. It's important to note that the way the groom turns, their tone of voice, and their hand and face gestures all come into play, but that will come naturally with proper planning of the groom's speech. That's why you are reading this!

Get your pen and paper ready, you're about to start writing your speech.

Chapter Four

Welcome and general opening of your speech

I opened my speech with:

- *"Good afternoon everyone! We take great pleasure in welcoming you here for our special day... where the countdown is over... and we are now Mr & Mrs >**surname**<! (pause for applause!)"*

By saying 'Mr and Mrs >**surname**<' you will evoke a big cheer and definitely get a reaction. Some guests will have been at hundreds of weddings, and will be well versed as to when to cheer and whoop! I continued:

- *"On behalf of my wife and I (!!!) We want to thank you all for being here with us on this special day, for all your good wishes, and for your wonderful gifts. People have travelled from various parts of the UK to be with us today... we have large groups of people from Cornwall and Devon, Essex and London, and the Midlands, among others".*

This will recognize the distances some have travelled, and if you pause at the end of saying each town/city and look up at the audience, you will invariably get cheers and noise from those who have travelled from those areas! Without sounding too technical here, this tactic builds rapport and gets the guests involved in a positive way. Mentioning 'my wife and I' will always get a merry cheer from those seasoned guests who have been eager for this phrase to be said!

Another popular way for most grooms to open their speech is to thank the father of the bride for his kind words. It was slightly different for my wedding speech, as my 'father of the bride' speech was before the meal and there were some time between the two. I go on to say my thanks for the previous speech later. You may choose to thank the father of the bride at this point, especially if they have just spoken and he has just handed you the microphone.

- *"For a while we've looked forward to bringing all the people that are special to us together, and now you're here, all scrubbed up and smelling nice. It's surreal for me to speak to you all at the same time. The fact that you are all here means everything to us.*

- *Just a bit of housekeeping – please make sure your glasses are charged for any toasts. Please stay in your seats for toasts from me – just raising a glass is fine! I have a few gifts to hand out later so when I do, a big clap would be great please!"*

It's a good idea to instruct the guests as to what to do; it saves any awkwardness and the more nervous guests regarding correct etiquette will have been briefed! Also, while we are talking about toasts, it's obvious but please remember to say the toasts loudly and exactly as you want them to be heard. For example, *"A toast please, to, THE BRIDESMAIDS!"*

This will give your guests the cue to do the same. I have been to some weddings where this hasn't been done, and the speaker has just raised a glass and drank, leaving the guests unsure and mumbling their own version of a toast. It looks and sounds, for want of a better word, unprofessional. Also with regard to toasts, telling the guests whether to stand up or sit down is important. Remember, as much as you may not want to be, you need to direct the guests to do as you ask. You don't have to be formal about this, you could say, *"to save the musical chairs, I'd like you to..."*.

I used bullet points to not merge my separate statements; you could of course always shorten these. As I have mentioned, I read out all my points in full, which got my words across exactly as I had intended. It is up to you whether to go into as much detail as I have.

Chapter Five

Thanks to new in-laws

This part of your speech should give thanks to your new in-laws for welcoming you into the family. Now is your opportunity to show your appreciation to the bride's family for being so kind and caring. With most families this is the case, but feel free to amend your speech if it is not!

For my speech, it was actually my wife's mother who spoke before me and did the speech of 'father of the bride', due to my wife's father having passed away when she was younger. I made reference to this in my speech and made appropriate toasts later in my speech. You will work out how to structure this for yourself based on my layout below.

- *"I would like to thank >**mother of bride**< and >**mother of the bride's partner**< for making me feel a part of the family since day one, and I must thank >mother of the bride< for her kind words before the meal! You have always been an inspiration to me, to in your words 'never lose your sparkle'. It's clear to us all that >**bride**< and >**bride's sister**< have been fantastically brought up. You have been a rock to them both and you are clearly a very special lady. I am proud that I now officially have a second mum!"*

You may choose to then go on with an interesting anecdote about your induction into the family, or how you met. Mine was as follows:

- *"We holidayed as 'family >**family surname (e.g. Smith)**<' in Florida in the summer of 2012 .... It was incredible! One incident made me think I was truly part of the family.... (Mention the theme park and breaking the wine bottles in the evening – hope they have forgiven me!).*

- *>**mother of bride**< - You, >**mother of the bride's partner**< and >**bride's sister**< have all made me feel so welcome since the beginning and I am so lucky to have married your daughter today, who is the most beautiful person to me in every sense. I'd also like to say how wonderful both you and my own mum look today, and I'm sure everyone else agrees! (*cue cheers/whoops).*

- *I would now like us now to raise a toast to >**bride's**< father, >**bride's father (who is no longer with us)**<. Although I never had the pleasure of meeting him, I am told we are alike in many ways and I hope he would have approved of >**bride's**< choice of husband. I know he would be very, very proud of you. A toast please... to >**bride's father (who is no longer with us)**<. Thank you all.*

- *To Mum, Dad, >**mother of bride**< and >**mother of the bride's partner**<, Thank you* *for everything you've done towards making today a success. We really appreciate you being there for us and we wanted to give you a little something to thank you. *Hand presents*. A round of applause please for our family.*

Chapter Six

Thanks to own mother and father

This chapter will give you an opportunity to thank your own parents for everything they have done for you, not only for the wedding but also in your life so far. Of course, you can be the judge of what detail to go in here. It is always a nice touch to reveal a little about your upbringing, your relationship with your parents, and some anecdotes about your brothers and sisters. As you will see, I've put some personal detail in my speech that most will know to be true already (that I like rugby and I am also from Cornwall). The majority of guests will know you well and be able to identify with the things you say. Try to keep it general, with a few universally appreciated stories that every guest will relate to. Here is what I wrote:

- *"Personally now, I'd like to say a thank you to my wonderful parents or, as I like to say in my strongest Cornish accent, **motheeeeer** and **faaather**! I owe so much to you both, all the evenings and the long trips to hundreds of rugby pitches across the country in my youth, and generally for kicking me out of bed in time for school.*

- *Dad- you have been an inspiration to me with your work ethic and drive to develop the business and you have put in some crazy hours, I still don't know how you got by with as little sleep! When I was a toddler Dad used to make me hot chocolate at 5.30am each morning before going to work. I am thankful for you and mum giving me the opportunity to pursue my passions of rugby and sport, which has led to a career in these fields.*

- *Mum, as I've said, you look amazing today. My main aim with this bit is to make you cry! You have always been the caring, rational, supportive and loving person watching over me and helping me with anything, from washing rugby kit, to your help with certain school projects. You too are an inspiration in so many ways. Thank you for everything.*

You can make this section as personal as you like. Some wish to simply say 'thank you' in a sentence, others will see it as an opportunity to publically say how much they appreciate their parents' contribution.

Chapter Seven

Thanks to maid of honour and bridesmaids

I started this section with:

- *"Now with ladies first, I would like to continue in traditional fashion by thanking our maid of honour, >bride's< sister, >bride's sister's name< and all of our bridesmaids. I know you'll (addressing audience) all agree that they all look beautiful!" (cue some whooping and clapping by lifting the tone of your voice at the end of the sentence).*

By saying you would like to be traditional in your speech structure implies respect and gentlemanly conduct, and is respectful of the formality of the speech. The best speeches I have ever seen in any situation acknowledge the formalities of the situation. If you want it to be less overtly formal than I was above, you could simply say, "I would like to say thanks to…".

I continued:

- *">Bride's sister< (also Maid of honour), you have always been with >bride< in both the good times **and** the tough times as her sister, and always been there for **us** both with advice, support and a lot of laughs. Thanks for everything you have done for us (including for our wedding), you have put in a great deal of work that we both appreciate. Also, to the*

> *bridesmaids >**Bridesmaid 1**< (my sister), >**Bridesmaid 2**< and >**Bridesmaid 3**<, thanks for all of your support for >**bride**<, she loves each of you dearly, and we value each of you immensely.*

- *>**Bridesmaid 1**<, 'sis', even though I still think you are 12 (and I still treat you like you're 12!!!), you have grown up into a beautiful young lady. Now you, >**bride**< and >**bride's sister**< are officially sisters! Ahh!*

- *We hope you enjoyed opening your gifts this morning with >**bride**<. A toast please… to… the bridesmaids!"*

Feel free to insert any anecdotes about a funny story. If you're in any doubt (with regard to making a remark about the bridal party), leave it out. If you mention anything mildly controversial (for comic effect) that is not flattering, always conclude on a heartfelt and genuine note to ensure you come across as being sincere and genuine in your affections. Doing this will be powerful and will mitigate any funny stories you may tell about them! They will have all put in a huge amount of effort in to the wedding preparations and to how they look on the day, so it will always go down well to thank and appreciate them for this. Remember, if in doubt, leave it out!

Chapter Eight

Thanks to groom's party

Having thanked the bridesmaids, you now have the license to be a lot more light-hearted when talking about your own ushers and best man! You may feel yourself loosening up and getting more comfortable in your speech, and now is where you can take it to a new level in terms of warmth and humor. As with the bridesmaids, any light hearted comment or funny story should be immediately followed by a genuine and heartfelt word of appreciation for your closest friends. If you do this, the recipient of the initial joke will know that you genuinely care, and haven't just taken advantage of them for comic effect. It is a chance to say genuinely nice things about them (which you may not do to their face all that often!).

Here's how I did it:

- *"Onto my groom's party today. They are all here for their companionship; clearly not for their brains or beauty!"*

A friendly comment like this isn't always necessary but I thought it was appropriate for my lot! I go on to say:

- *">**Best man<**, thanks for everything you have done in preparation for today, including an incredible stag do in >**place name<**. >**Best man<**, we go back to our primary school days playing football against each other for >**school*** *name<! We were part of the infamous backstreet boys tribute dance group in a school concert **(addressing audience)** - I am still as shocked as you lot are! We have been solid mates for a long time. We may not have seen each other as much as we'd have liked to because of where we've lived recently.... but whenever we meet up it is as if no time has passed. (Addressing audience) Believe it or not, >**Best man**< has worked as a manager for L'Oréal shampoo. I'd like to say thanks for being my best man by giving you a little something too. Because you're worth it. Cheers mate". ***Hand present***.*

You will have a story of how you met your best man or even one where he has been a fool, so you could always use this before praising him and thanking him for his efforts. I continued:

- *"Thanks also to my ushers- my brother >**Usher 1**<, then there's >**Usher 2**< and >**Usher 3**<. You guys have been fantastic not only today but throughout my life as mates".*

You could choose to keep it brief and leave it here, as this so far would suffice as a bare minimum. I chose to thank my groom's party in more detail as I felt the audience would enjoy it and I would like to take the opportunity to publically recognize them.

- *>**Usher 1, also my brother**<, it means so much that you could be my usher today. I want to thank you for always being there to support me and scrap with me (and beat me up many times). You watched over me like a hawk as I cut the lawn (as* *a quality assurance measure of course), and generally looked after all things in the business when dad went 'gallivanting' on his rugby away days (*turn to dad* you still do that don't you?). A 3 hour trip to where we live is apparently 'do-able in a day!'. >Usher 1<, we had some great times growing up spending days out with cousins (all of which are here today!) with Granny, Grampy, Granddad and our <u>amazing</u> Grandma and Auntie Sylvia. Hi Grandma and Auntie Sylvia! >Usher 1<, you have been caring and kind - >bride< loves the fact she now has a brother! *Hand present*.*

- *>Usher 2<, when you arrived at >secondary school name< in Year 9... with long blonde golden locks (*audience should now laugh as he is now bald*).... you were the quickest kid on a rugby pitch I had ever seen, and had a thick northern accent. Where's that gone!? We had some great times throughout school, at Uni and ever since then. You can all ask >Usher 2< later to see pictures of his infamous 'dreadlock' phase. It will be well worth it I promise you! Please accept my gift as a thank you. *Hand present*.*

- *>Usher 3<, you've been there since I started working at >insert workplace< – you and >insert girlfriend's name< have been great friends to >bride< and I. You have always been there at the drop of a hat, and along with >other colleague< and >other colleague< you have made sure I have stayed sane at work – and made sure that I have a laugh too! Not only have <u>we</u> enjoyed your company, but we have a golden Labrador who* *also loves you very much! (It's a good job too, because you're the one that convinced us to get him!). Please may I give you a little something for being my usher today. ***Hand Present****

- *A toast please, to ... the groom's party".*

Chapter Nine

Thanks to pageboys, flower girls and venue

If you have them at your wedding, now is the time to thank the pageboys and flower girls. I said:

- *"May I also say a big thanks to our beautiful flower girls for helping us today! >flower girl 1<, >flower girl 2< and >flower girl 3<.... you all look amazing. A round of applause please for the flower girls! We are so happy that we have altogether so many children at our wedding; you really make it special as we've got to know each of you and seen you grow up!".*

We chose to include a brief thanks for our venue and caterers as we felt they did a fantastic job. It is polite to, but not essential. I give a brief anecdote below:

- *"We wanted to thank the >venue name< for hosting our wedding today. We've been in awe of the place since we first saw it! Also thanks to >catering company name<, our amazing caterers today. That roast beef was amazing! By the way, we went to a 'taster' day to 'sample' our food - I had one of those joints to myself and I couldn't breathe after!!! In appreciation for both our venue and caterers please could we give a round of applause".*

Chapter Ten

Speech about your wife

Now the main formalities are said and done, the last and most important part of your speech is to say a heartfelt piece about your beautiful wife. This is the most important part of the speech and is what people will remember the speech for. It is a big opportunity to tell the world how much she means to you. This should be the part you put the most thought into. Please note, my section about my wife was probably on the long side, but I felt it was completely worth it as it was my time to say what I felt about her to all the friends and family that were listening. You could, for your speech, shorten this section considerably. It should be a minimum of about three or four sentences. I started:

- *"Most importantly today, I wanted to thank >**Bride's new, full married name**< for agreeing to marry me! As >**mother of the bride**< has already said, she is beautiful, she's kind, she's caring and loving... and I still can't believe how lucky I am to now be able to call her my wife!*

Most audiences will at least give an 'Ahh' or at most give a round of applause. If this happens, let it! Enjoy the moment and don't rush through it. I continued:

- ***addressing bride*** *>**bride**<, "I want to take this moment to share some of our story so far* with everyone. *(addressing audience) Don't panic!*

- *We met through mutual friends at University in mid 2008, as fresh faced 21 year olds! When we met we were in the final year and, nights out with our own friends usually ended up at >**insert nightclub/bar**<. I'd been introduced to >**bride**< before but proceeded to bump into her and not have anything else to say (or shout) but, "Hi, alright??? How you doing??". What a natural, must get it from my father! I knew I wanted to speak to you and get to know you, but I had nothing else in my conversational locker than that. I thought then, and I still think, >**bride**< is 100% the most beautiful girl I have ever seen. She is the most beautiful person not just because she's stunning, but because she is the most caring, considerate, trustworthy and thoughtful person around, which I am sure you'll all agree. As I like to call her, she's a free range, good egg. She always puts others before herself and that's why she has so many close friends ... and that's why so many people want to be friends with her. After a few awkward conversations and impromtu passings by, **I asked** >**bride**< **out** (to see >**insert film title**< at the cinema). We soon knew our personalities were well and truly matched... and I could tell we were onto a winner. I took >**bride**< as my girlfriend to the May ball in 2009 at university (With >**university friends**<- great memories guys!). I was so proud of being with you and couldn't* *believe how lucky I was! Since then the rest is history, but history that I will briefly detail.*

- *For two years we lived 263 miles apart while boyfriend and girlfriend (so was the distance between >**city name**< and >**city name**<). After many train journeys from us both, >**bride**< made the decision to come down to >**city name**< to live with me and work while I pursued my rugby career. After a year we took the leap of faith and went... as I would call it.... **'up north'.** At least for a Cornish lad it was **'up north'**! We've been lucky to spend a lot of time seeing more of >**bride's**< Midlands-based family in the last 3 years, particularly **nanny! Hi Nan!***

- *We have also met (and got to know) some fantastic people over the last 3 years from our Midlands base. I've mentioned >**insert colleague's names**< for me..... now I can include for us both: >**insert friends' names**<.*

- *We have a brilliant life together in Solihull with Jelly the cat, and more recently joined by Max the dog and Ripley the horse. Our horse doesn't live with us... but >**bride**< wishes he did.*

- *Some of you may not know that >**bride**< and I have lived parallel lives. We were born on the same day so we share the same birthday (on >**insert date**< – born only 7 hours apart). >**Bride**< is older -I think I've caught up in height since! We had our appendix out at the same time before we knew each other aged 19. These are just two of the coincidences that are freakishly similar between us.*

- *>**Bride**<, I love you with all my heart and you are, as my nickname for you suggests, in every sense, 'gorgeous'. You are my soulmate and I can't begin to think of my life without you in it! Your generosity and your selflessness is on a level unlike any other person I have ever met. You're supportive, caring, loving, ...and I can't wait for us to continue our lives together as husband and wife.*

- *Now... A toast please ... to the gorgeous, >**bride's full married name**<!"*

Chapter Eleven

Introduction of best man

Congratulations - you have nearly planned your wedding speech! The last act for you to do is now introduce the best man as he prepares for his speech. You *could* simply introduce him by name; but remember - this is an opportunity to informally introduce him as a good mate, and warn the guests of what rubbish he is about to talk! Traditionally, the best man will start his speech with formalities then cut to the chase of embarrassing you as much as possible.

- *"Now, I'd like to take a moment to introduce your next speaker, my best man, >**insert best man's name**<. I've flattered him so far, and his ego may be slightly inflated. For those who are fans of the TV show Bad Education - he is the embodiment of Alfie Wickers (a slapstick character on British TV). .....For those familiar with children's TV he is your poor man's Mr Tumble (another slapstick character on British TV).*

I knew that he had done a degree in journalism which led me to construct the last part of my speech.

- *He is currently, by profession, a maths teacher, but believe it or not his undergraduate degree is in broadcast journalism! So you now all know....... not to believe a word he says!!! Thank you and have a great day everyone!* ***hands microphone over to best man***.

The last bullet point, where I reveal my best man was a journalist, was amazing ammunition for this joke. But here's the thing, you can use it too with the correct wording/delivery. You could always adapt this for anyone who hasn't done a journalism degree by saying (insinuating) that the best man once worked for a specific tabloid paper. Even though it's not necessarily true, it makes the joke work!

The upside to finishing on a joke is that you can say, "thank you everyone!" at the end of your speech, and as you are handing the microphone over people will take that as a cue to give applause. It's a natural way of handing over on your terms, and be the perfect nudge for the guests to clap. You could put a completely different joke in to do with the fact that your best man has a habit of lying or stretching the truth, or at the least simply introduce him by name and then add, "I hope he is kind to me now!"

Chapter Twelve

Wedding day advice for the groom

You have now planned your speech (or are about to do so), and you are getting ready for the day. Whether it is two years away or two days away, I would like to pass on some advice for soon-to-be husbands for the day itself.

In the lead up to the day you will have sent invitations, designed seating plans and deliberated over the guest list. You will have spoken to the catering company and will have the venue host's number on speed dial. You will have done your best to, with your wife, plan the best possible celebration of your marriage. Your speech will only enhance your reputation within both families and the fact you have prepared it so well will mean so much to a lot of people. The focus of a wedding is traditionally on the bride, the dress, and the food – yet nobody actually tells you, the groom, how to prepare yourself for the day. I will reveal what it was like from my point of view as the groom, to give you a heads-up.

I recommend getting to know your photographer and meeting up in advance of the wedding day. I appreciate you may think this unnecessary, but it's totally worth it in terms of how your photos come out.

Most wedding photographers will offer a pre-wedding shoot package which not only allows you both to get used to the camera, but also get to know how your photographer operates to make images seem as natural as possible. Our photographer Rob gave us simple stances and poses to make sure that on the day we were able to go on auto-pilot when he was there.

My wife and I did do a pre-wedding shoot. We are both naturally introverted, and the pre-shoot made us feel really comfortable on our wedding day. We also managed to get some great pictures of us (and our dog!) at a beautiful National Trust site that we could keep forever.

The day before your wedding you will hopefully have some quiet family time once the essentials are in place. The decorations will be put up, your suit laid out ready for the big day, and your nearest and dearest will be starting to arrive. You will have a lot of people ask you how you are feeling. They will ask, "*how you are coping?*". They ask with the best intentions (to appear supportive), but some ask with the assumption that it is only a matter of time before you have a nervous moment or a breakdown - which may not be the case until they ask the question! Take it in your stride and don't let other people make you feel stressed or pressured. Keep calm within yourself and look forward to the things you are most looking forward to.

It's important to get an early night. Make it a priority, as you will be up and entertaining guests for over twelve hours the following day. I have heard horror stories of grooms that have gone for a 'quiet few' drinks the night before and have been horrendously tender the morning of their wedding. Pre-decide on a bed time, stick to it, and don't have an excessive amount of alcohol. You will need a clear head and you won't want your memories of your wedding morning to be tainted by a huge hangover!

You will more than likely be staying separate from your fiancé the night before the wedding, so playing computer games or spending time with friends is a good idea. This will keep your mind occupied without over-exerting yourself!

In the morning, you will probably get ready with all of your groom's party. It may seem obvious, but make sure you eat all pre-ceremony food in your regular clothes to save spillages on your wedding suits! This seems common sense but on the day it could be a disastrous mistake. The bridal party may take all morning to get ready - some brides get up at 6am for hair and make-up. You probably won't get up this early, but make sure you allow enough time to do things you will only do on your wedding day. Set aside time for the fiddly bits and pieces such as putting on button-hole flowers, fitting your cuff links and tying your tie (I needed to go on YouTube to learn how to tie a Windsor knot!). Doing these things last minute is not ideal and is not what you need to occupy your mind with.

The beginning of the day is essentially coordinated by the groom and the groom's party, as they are expected to greet the hired personnel such as the caterers and photographers, as well as the guests. I would advise you decide well before the day what roles your ushers and best man should have on the morning of your wedding so you don't have to worry about them. For example, ask your best man to speak to the venue host first thing, and ask an usher to take care of the photographer. Prepare them for these roles, and they will know what is required of them.

Your registrar or church service will usually conduct separate meetings with the bride and groom an hour or two before the wedding ceremony, to prove your identities and that you are legally able to wed. Don't be alarmed by any direct questioning, as they can be blunt and to the point. Once this formality is over, the ceremony will be along soon.

I know a lot of guests take the entrance of the bride as an opportunity to watch for the groom's reaction! You will obviously be delighted to see each other after a day or so apart, so remember to smile and get ready to enjoy the ceremony!

When the ceremony ends, make sure you have already allocated someone to work with the photographer and have a list prepared of all the different wedding shots you want. If left to chance, it will be a long-winded process and can lead to frustration if it's cold outside! Try to make this as quick and efficient as possible. Assigning an usher or the best man to work with the photographer is always a great idea.

Throughout the day, you will want to talk at length with all of your guests. Depending on how big your guest list is, you may simply not have enough time, so don't worry if you can't catch up with everybody. You will be able to catch up in the weeks/months after with your closest friends, so try to prioritise seeing those you don't see very often, like family and friends who have travelled long distances. If you want to see as many people as possible, you can limit yourself to a few minutes per guest, having a 'closing line' such as, "it's lovely to see you, thanks for coming, I must say hello to X & Y". Guests know you will be in demand and won't be offended by your brevity.

Don't build up your speech more than you need to. You may find yourself dwelling on it or getting daunted, but remember, you have prepared excellently and are completely ready! It is worth reading it to groomsmen or your fiancé a week or two before (minus the parts about them!) to sound out any minor things that need to be changed or added. I know some grooms who wrote their speech the night before on a scrap of paper or even hurriedly on the day. This is far from ideal if you want to impress! Doing this can make your speech seem rushed, you will not be confident and it will be something you had wished you had put more time into.

There is some down time between a traditional wedding breakfast and the evening guests arriving. During this time I suggest you and your new wife take a minute to have a cup of tea or relax! You will have had a very busy day and you will appreciate some time together to take it all in and settle down. I would suggest planning this in otherwise you won't do it. Trust me, just taking twenty minutes to relax will refresh you both and enable you to look forward to the rest of the evening even more!

Cutting the cake is an awkward formality and a rite of passage that most married couples are subjected to. It feels very awkward and it is just one of the photo opportunities that guests love, so just smile and wave! Also, make a point of having some evening food; you will be surprised at how easily your time can be taken up by others who want to wish you well! You will have carefully selected the dining options for your guests; so why shouldn't you take some time to enjoy it for yourselves?

The first dance is something you may wish to practice together. However, my advice is that it is completely unnecessary unless you particularly want to show something off, or if you are, unlike me, very good at dancing! It is perfectly acceptable to sway slowly around the dancefloor, there is no need to do anything elaborate.

The evening will go very quickly, so it will be up to you to get the right balance between mingling with your close friends and those who you do not often see. You will feel like you are on official duties, but remember to enjoy yourself! The day is should be enjoyed for every minute, and is the first day of your new lives together. Make sure you soak it all up, and take some moments to step back and reflect on the spectacle you and your partner have created. I'm sure that you'll have the best day of your lives.

Chapter Thirteen

Extra Jokes you could use

Although I did not use these jokes in my speech, these are some of the best ones I left on the cutting room floor. I have heard these across all the weddings I have ever been to. You may find they come in handy, so take your pick if you wish!

- With regard to any obvious accidents or mishaps throughout the day so far: *"Well, I'm glad the RAC were able to sort out the 1937 Austin Healey bridal car! The coughing fit from the woman who signed the register wasn't distracting at all, was it >**bride**<?"*

- *"For a good speech I'm told the speaker needs to stand up to be seen, speak up to be heard, and sit down and shut up!"*

- Props can be used if there's a time and a place for them. I know some have got out their new wife's oldest and most favourite teddy bear, and follow it with saying something like, *"I hope I can live up to your clearly high standards as a life partner!"*

- *(on being nervous) I'm so nervous; you'll have to forgive me. Even my speech is sponsored by Jim and Beam!*

- *(On the best man/ushers)* – *"My ushers and best man all did a runner last night – so I'd like to introduce their stand-ins!"*

- *(On the best man/ushers)* – *"They are all dressed so smartly because they've just come here straight from court this morning".*

- *Now, William Shakespeare was once quoted as saying, "If music be the food of love, then play on". Lovely, but have you seen Dad's dancing?! There's an exception to every rule.*

- One that's always gone down well is the use of the bride or best man's old school report (or a scrap of paper that pretends to be!). You could relate their interests to their old subjects at school to get a laugh.

- *(To new in-laws)* *"A lot of men have said they've had a bad experience with getting to know their new in-laws, but I have gained the perfect second set of parents. I couldn't be happier. (*looks to in-laws) Maggie and Bob, did I read that OK?"*

Chapter Fourteen

Steve's speech in full

- *"Good afternoon everyone! We take great pleasure in welcoming you here for our special day... where the countdown is over... and we are now Mr & Mrs >**surname**<! (pause for applause!)"*

- *"On behalf of my wife and I (!!!) we want to thank you all for being here with us on this special day, for all your good wishes, and for your wonderful gifts. People have travelled from various parts of the UK to be with us today... we have large groups of people from Cornwall and Devon, Essex and London, and the Midlands, among others".*

- *"For a while we've looked forward to bringing all the people that are special to us together, and now you're here, all scrubbed up and smelling nice. It's surreal for me to speak to you all at the same time. The fact that you are all here means everything to us.*

- *Just a bit of housekeeping – please make sure your glasses are charged for any toasts. Please stay in your seats for toasts from me – just raising a glass is fine! I have a few gifts to hand out later so when I do, a big clap would be great please!"*
  - *"We holidayed as 'family >**family surname (e.g. Smith)**<' in Florida in the summer of 2012 .... it was incredible! One incident made me think I was truly part of the family....*

(mention the theme park and breaking the wine bottles in the evening – hope they have forgiven me!).

- *>**mother of bride**< - You, >**mother of the bride's partner**< and >**bride's sister**< have all made me feel so welcome since the beginning and I am so lucky to have married your daughter today, who is the most beautiful person to me in every sense. I'd also like to say how wonderful both you and my own mum look today, and I'm sure everyone else agrees! (*cue cheers/whoops).*

- *I would now like us now to raise a toast to >**bride's**< father, >**bride's father (who is no longer with us)**<. Although I never had the pleasure of meeting him, I am told we are alike in many ways and I hope he would have approved of >**bride's**< choice of husband. I know he would be very, very proud of you. A toast please... to >**bride's father (who is no longer with us)**<. Thank you all.*

- *To Mum, Dad, >**mother of bride**< and >**mother of the bride's partner**<, Thank you for everything you've done towards making today a success. We really appreciate you being there for us and we wanted to give you a little something to thank you. *Hand presents*. A round of applause please for our family.*

- *"Personally now, I'd like to say a thank you to my wonderful parents or, as I like to say in my strongest Cornish accent,* **motheeeeer** *and* **faaather***! I owe so much to you both, all the evenings and the long trips to hundreds of rugby pitches across the country in my youth, and generally for kicking me out of bed in time for school.*

- *Dad- you have been an inspiration to me with your work ethic and drive to develop the business and you have put in some crazy hours, I still don't know how you got by with as little sleep! When I was a toddler Dad used to make me hot chocolate at 5.30am each morning before going to work. I am thankful for you and mum giving me the opportunity to pursue my passions of rugby and sport, which has led to a career in these fields.*

- *Mum, as I've said, you look amazing today. My main aim with this bit is to make you cry! You have always been the caring, rational, supportive and loving person watching over me and helping me with anything, from washing rugby kit, to your help with certain school projects. You too are an inspiration in so many ways. Thank you for everything.*

- *"Now with ladies first, I would like to continue in traditional fashion by thanking our maid of honour, >**bride's**< sister, >**bride's sister's name**< and all of our bridesmaids. I know you'll (**addressing audience**) all agree* *that they all look beautiful!" (cue some whooping and clapping by lifting the tone of your voice at the end of the sentence).*

- **">Bride's sister< (also Maid of honour)**, *you have always been with >bride< in both the good times __and__ the tough times as her sister, and always been there for __us__ both with advice, support and a lot of laughs. Thanks for everything you have done for us (including for our wedding), you have put in a great deal of work that we both appreciate. Also, to the bridesmaids >**Bridesmaid 1**< (my sister), >**Bridesmaid 2**< and >**Bridesmaid 3**<, thanks for all of your support for >bride<, she loves each of you dearly, and we value each of you immensely.*

- >**Bridesmaid 1**<, *'sis', even though I still think you are 12 (and I still treat you like you're 12!!!), you have grown up into a beautiful young lady. Now you, >**bride**< and >**bride's sister**< are officially sisters! Ahh!*

- *We hope you enjoyed opening your gifts this morning with >**bride**<. A toast please... to... the bridesmaids!"*

- *"Onto my groom's party today. They are all here for their companionship; clearly not for their brains or beauty!"*

- ">*Best man*<, *thanks for everything you have done in preparation for today, including an incredible stag do in >place name<. >Best man<, we go back to our primary school days playing football against each other for >school name<! We were part of the infamous backstreet boys tribute dance group in a school concert (**addressing audience**) - I am still as shocked as you lot are! We have been solid mates for a long long time. We may not have seen each other as much as we'd have liked to because of where we've lived recently.... but whenever we meet up it is as if no time has passed. (Addressing audience) Believe it or not, >Best man< has worked as a manager for L'Oréal shampoo. I'd like to say thanks for being my best man by giving you a little something too. Because you're worth it. Cheers mate". *Hand present*.*

- "Thanks also to my ushers- my brother >**Usher 1**<, then there's >**Usher 2**< and >**Usher 3**<. You guys have been fantastic not only today but throughout my life as mates".*

- >**Usher 1, also my brother**<, it means so much that you could be my usher today. I want to thank you for always being there to support me and scrap with me (and beat me up many times).You watched over me like a hawk as I cut the lawn (as a quality assurance measure of course), and generally looked after all things in the business when dad went 'gallivanting' on his rugby away days (*turn to dad* you still do that don't you?).*

A 3 hour trip to where we live is apparently 'do-able in a day!'. **>Usher 1<**, *we had some great times growing up spending days out with cousins (all of which are here today!) with Granny, Grampy, Granddad and our <u>amazing</u> Grandma and Auntie Sylvia. Hi Grandma and Auntie Sylvia!* **>Usher 1<**, *you have been caring and kind -* **>bride<** *loves the fact she now has a brother!* ***Hand present*.**

- **>Usher 2<**, *when you arrived at* **>secondary school name<** *in Year 9... with long blonde golden locks* **(*audience should now laugh as he is now bald*)**.... *you were the quickest kid on a rugby pitch I had ever seen, and had a thick northern accent. Where's that gone!? We had some great times throughout school, at Uni and ever since then. You can all ask* **>Usher 2<** *later to see pictures of his infamous 'dreadlock' phase. It will be well worth it I promise you! Please accept my gift as a thanks.* ***Hand present*.**

- **>Usher 3<**, *you've been there since I started working at* **>insert workplace<** *– you and* **>insert girlfriend's name<** *have been great friends to* **>bride<** *and I. You have always been there at the drop of a hat, and along with* **>other colleague<** *and* **>other colleague<** *you have made sure I have stayed sane at work – and made sure that I have a laugh too! Not only have <u>we</u> enjoyed your company, but we have a golden Labrador who also loves you very much! (good job too, because you're the one that convinced us to get him!). Please may I give you a little something for being my usher today.* ***Hand Present***

- *A toast please to ... the groom's party".*

  - *"May I also say a big thanks to our beautiful flower girls for helping us today! >flower girl 1<, >flower girl 2< and >flower girl 3<.... you all look amazing. A round of applause please for the flower girls! We are so happy that we have altogether so many children at our wedding; you really make it special as we've got to know each of you and seen you grow up!".*

  - *"We wanted to thank the >venue name< for hosting our wedding today. We've been in awe of the place since we first saw it! Also thanks to >catering company name<, our amazing caterers today. That roast beef was amazing! By the way, we went to a 'taster' day to 'sample' our food - I had one of those joints to myself and I couldn't breathe after!!! In appreciation for both our venue and caterers please could we give a round of applause".*

  - *"Most importantly today, I wanted to thank >Bride's new, full married name< for agreeing to marry me! As >mother of the bride< has already said, she is beautiful, she's kind, she's caring and loving... and I still can't believe how lucky I am to now be able to call her my wife!*

  - ***addressing bride* >bride<, I want to take this moment to share some of our story so far* with everyone. *(addressing audience) Don't panic!*

- *We met through mutual friends at University in mid 2008, as fresh faced 21 year olds! When we met we were in the final year and, nights out with our own friends usually ended up at >**insert nightclub/bar**<. I'd been introduced to >**bride**< before but proceeded to bump into her and not have anything else to say (or shout) but, "Hi, alright??? How you doing??". What a natural, must get it from my father! I knew I wanted to speak to you and get to know you, but I had nothing else in my conversational locker than that. I thought then, and I still think, >**bride**< is 100% the most beautiful girl I have ever seen. She is the most beautiful person not just because she's stunning, but because she is the most caring, considerate, trustworthy and thoughtful person around, which I am sure you'll all agree. As I like to call her, she's a free range, good egg. She always puts others before herself and that's why she has so many close friends ... and that's why so many people want to be friends with her. After a few awkward conversations and impromtu passings by, <u>**I asked**</u> >**bride**< <u>**out**</u> (to see >**insert film title**< at the cinema). We soon knew our personalities were well and truly matched... and I could tell we were onto a winner. I took >**bride**< as my girlfriend to the May ball in 2009 at university (With >**university friends**<- great memories guys!). I was so proud of being with you and couldn't* *believe how lucky I was! Since then the rest is history, but history that I will briefly detail.*

- *For two years we lived 263 miles apart while boyfriend and girlfriend (so was the distance between >**city name**< and >**city name**<). After many train journeys from us both, >**bride**< made the decision to come down to >**city name**< to live with me and work while I pursued my rugby career. After a year we took the leap of faith and went... as I would call it.... **'up north'.** At least for a Cornish lad it was **'up north'**! We've been lucky to spend a lot of time seeing more of >**bride's**< Midlands-based family in the last 3 years, particularly **nanny! Hi Nan!***

- *We have also met (and got to know) some fantastic people over the last 3 years from our Midlands base. I've mentioned >**insert colleague's names**< for me..... now I can include for us both: >**insert friends' names**<.*

- *We have a brilliant life together in Solihull with Jelly the cat, and more recently joined by Max the dog and Ripley the horse. Our horse doesn't live with us... but >**bride**< wishes he did.*

- *Some of you may not know that >**bride**< and I have lived parallel lives. We were born on the same day so we share the same birthday (on >**insert date**< – born only 7 hours apart). >**Bride**< is older -I think I've caught up in height since! We had our appendix out at the same time before we knew each other aged 19. These are just two of the coincidences that are freakishly similar between us.*

- *>**Bride**<, I love you with all my heart and you are, as my nickname for you suggests, in every sense, 'gorgeous'. You are my soulmate and I can't begin to think of my life without you in it! Your generosity and your selflessness is on a level unlike any other person I have ever met. You're supportive, caring, loving, ...and I can't wait for us to continue our lives together as husband and wife.*

- *Now... A toast please ... to the gorgeous, >**bride's full married name**<!*

- *"Now, I'd like to take a moment to introduce your next speaker, my best man, >**insert best man's name**<. I've flattered him so far, and his ego may be slightly inflated. For those who are fans of the TV show Bad Education - he is the embodiment of Alfie Wickers (a slapstick character on British TV). .....For those familiar with children's TV he is your poor man's Mr Tumble (another slapstick character on British TV).*

- *He is currently, by profession, a maths teacher, but believe it or not his undergraduate degree is in broadcast journalism! So you now all know....... <u>not to believe a word he says</u>!!! Thank you and have a great day everyone!* ****hands microphone over to best man*****.

Printed in Great Britain
by Amazon